REPULSING RACISM

reflections on racism and the Irish

D1785539

by

Gretchen Fitzgerald

GRETCHEN FITZGERALD was born in India. She attended schools in India and Britain and first came to Ireland to take an honours degree in Philosophy and Economics at University College Cork. For the last number of years she has worked with APSO, the Agency for Personal Service Overseas, prior to which she worked with Dublin County Council, the (former) Health Education Bureau and Trócaire.

First Published in Ireland in 1992 by
Attic Press
4 Upper Mount Street
Dublin 2

British Library Cataloguing in Publication Data
Fitzgerald, Gretchen
    Repulsing Racism: reflections on racism and the Irish. -
(LIP Pamphlets Series)
    1. Title 11. Series
    305.3

ISBN 1-85594-034-5

Cover Design: Paula Nolan
Origination: Attic Press
Printing: Elo Press

Repulsing Racism

reflections on racism and the Irish

I have spent most of my life living in countries where I have been perceived, at least initially, as being different, often in a derogatory sense. For over forty years I have carried with me, like a dull ache, both the reality and the imminent possibility of being found unacceptable on the basis of culture and the colour of my skin. This has shaped and marked me. My perspective on racism in Ireland is personal, rooted in my own experience and in the knowledge I have gained from living in Ireland for more than twenty of those forty years.

I use the terms black and white for convenience, without specifying the diversity within these categories, though being of Asian origin, I obviously recognise it.

PREJUDICE AND DISCRIMINATION

Racial prejudice is prejudice against people who look, speak, dress, or behave differently from 'us' because of their ethnic origins or culture. We are all guilty of racial prejudice, whether we are Indian, Irish or European. Such prejudice is often based on ignorance or fear, particularly when there is little contact between people of different nations or ethnic groups. This frequently gives rise to a mythology of popular misconceptions and generalisations. We are all familiar with stereotypes in film and drama of the drunken Irishman or the inscrutable Chinese. Such prejudice has existed for centuries. With the advent of colonialism, racial prejudice evolved into an ideology of racism. The concept of superior and inferior races based on a hierarchy of skin colour was formulated. This was further compounded by the existing hierarchy of male superiority to female inferiority becoming 'rationalised' in theories based on perceptible differences between the sexes and the consequent division of labour and economic power.

RACISM: THE BACKGROUND

Between the sixteenth and nineteenth centuries, first the Portuguese and Spanish and then the Dutch and British, set out in search of new lands, colonising new territories in pursuit of wealth and cheap raw materials. (Human beings, as slaves, were included in the latter category.) The colonisers were motivated by the ever-increasing needs and appetites of Europe after the industrial revolution. Dazzled by the abundance of resources they found, they were blind to the already existing developed societies, the established trade links and the industries they came upon. Europeans destroyed the social fabric, culture and customs of communities in South America, Africa, Asia, the West Indies and the Pacific. Moral and spiritual approval for these activities was provided by the Christian churches. Hard work and service to the crown were made paramount virtues. The Christian churches followed the merchants and state servants into the colonised lands, adding their 'spiritual mission' of conversion (forced or otherwise) to the European process of 'civilising the savages'.

European institutions of various kinds - legislative, administrative and bureaucratic - were assumed to be infinitely superior to local ones, which they either replaced or were grafted on to. As the colonisers saw it, they needed to impose their institutions in order to better control the local populations and more efficiently organise the export of resources. It was considered to be in the interests of local communities to absorb and adapt to the new cultures, either voluntarily or by force. Through this process of political and economic power racism as an ideology evolved, supported by the work of writers, philosophers and scientists.

The eighteenth and particularly the nineteenth centuries gave rise to a plethora of theories to support the ideology of racism. These were based on the premise that 'white' people were biologically superior to people of any other colour. Ethnic groups were examined, evaluated and compared to the 'white' races. The shape of European skulls was declared to be more suited to intellectual thought. A crude hierarchy of races based on colour - white, yellow, brown, black - was defined and justified. Where colonial societies dominated indigenous

4

populations, the hierarchy was made more complex by the interweaving strands of race and gender, resulting in four other categories: white men; white women; black men, who threatened white women and dominated black women; black women, who were seen as powerless, subservient and acquiescent in their subservience to the other three categories.

Insisting that certain groups of people are mentally, morally and physically superior to others because of their skin colour or some other biological feature, in turn leads to the insidious categorising of individuals on the basis of their 'natural' type and origin. So if one is considering a Scandinavian and an Indian for the same job, one may conclude before ever meeting either of them, that the Scandinavian will be more efficient. Such bio-social theories contend that physical features and intellectual and moral capabilities are transferred genetically and dictate all the relevant characteristics and traits of individuals belonging to the 'natural' type group.

This categorising by 'known natural' type is applied to men and women also. Men are seen as physically stronger, and independent. Women are seen as the primary carers of the very young, dependent and more suited to domestic labour. Women perform domestic labour, not because it requires essentially feminine skills, but because historically and culturally specific roles have been attributed to women.

This thinking came to threaten Europeans themselves through fascism, the aim of which was to literally eliminate all those perceived to belong to inferior races. And it was only after the culmination of such thinking in the holocaust that the notion of biologically superior races became morally unjustifiable.

After the second world war, UNESCO gathered together a group of scientists to examine the issue of racial hierarchies. They concluded that race was more a social myth than a biological phenomenon. Certainly the human race is characterised more by its similarities than by the wealth of differences in skin colour and ethnic origin which are often mistakenly equated with 'race'.

5

But theories of biological superiority persist. Most of us have been brought up to believe that there are many different races, all biologically determined on the basis of real or perceived differences. From this it is but a small step to conclude that variations in physical features, culture and behaviour are based on innate biological differences. So, Irish people are all lazy, as are Africans, while Germans are cold! Such prejudiced generalisations, and categorising by racial or national typology, has further implications. Some white Europeans are considered to be inherently superior to all others. Friction and antagonism between 'superior' and 'inferior' nations therefore becomes inevitable. Yet the culture and beliefs of groups of people, even in countries which are ethnically homogeneous (and few are), have evolved over many centuries and were in process long before national boundaries were defined.

In 1965, the United Nations, in the *International Convention on the Elimination of All Forms of Racial Discrimination*, defined racism as 'any distinction, exclusion, restriction or preference based on race, colour, descent or national or ethnic origin ...' But words are not sufficient to remove feelings of superiority which have been lodged in the European psyche for generations or the reciprocal feeling of inferiority created in others. Only if existing global economic and power relations, established on the basis of racist thinking, are radically altered, will racist practices lose their attraction and diminish.

For me, the term racism denotes the relations of power by which one group dominates another because of ethnic or cultural differences. Racism is reinforced and combined with other forms of prejudice and discrimination based on class, gender and religion.

Whether we are the victims or the practitioners of racism (and each of us can find ourselves in either category at one time or another), we must change both our thinking and our behaviour in order to develop anti-racist practices. We need to monitor our conscious and unconscious attitudes if we are to bring about individual and collective change.

THE IRISH - VICTIMS AND PRACTITIONERS

Does racism exist in Ireland? Most Irish people if asked this question would tend to answer 'no'. They might also point out that the Irish have been and continue to be the victims of racial discrimination. As early as the seventeenth century plans were drawn up to make Ireland Britain's bread basket using Irish resources for the benefit, not of the nation, but of the British Crown. While historians disagree about the causes of the Famine (1845-48) certain facts remain. During each year of famine millions of pounds worth of food, mainly cattle and grain, were exported to Britain. Food was also imported and available to those who had the cash with which to purchase it. This situation in Ireland in the nineteenth century has its parallel in many third world countries today. (A term more accurate than 'third world' is people from Latin America, the Caribbean, Asia and the Pacific (LACAP). I have specifically used the term 'third world' here because, in the context of oppression and discrimination, the people of LACAP countries have been relegated to third place in the economic and political pecking order of global power.)

The Irish were considered by their British colonisers to be an inferior race and were regularly depicted as such in cartoons where they were compared to chimpanzees and 'blacks' and regarded as little better than 'savages'. Ireland is no longer a colony, but discrimination against the Irish in Britain, the United States and other countries to which the Irish have emigrated, is well documented. In Britain this persists in relation to accommodation, employment and social acceptance. The *No Irish Need Apply* signs were once as familiar to Irish emigrants as is the experience of black men and women in Ireland today being told that the flat is 'already let' when they look for accommodation, or the experience of black men, of being refused entry to discos in Dublin. Despite their history, the Irish abroad quickly realised that they could benefit from the situation of institutionalised white superiority by allying themselves with those in positions of dominance and took an active part in racial conflicts against other minorities in the United States and Australia. In recent years many Irish people have emigrated to South Africa. I still remember the day a college colleague excitedly told me of his plans to emigrate to South Africa,

7

without once acknowledging that by his action he would be openly supporting the apartheid regime.

Experiencing racism does not prevent one being racist oneself. This applies to the Irish at home and abroad at every level - individually, institutionally, and nationally. Irish society is predominantly white. It is often assumed to be monocultural, traditional, at ease with itself. Discontent, discrimination and oppression between rich and poor, men and women, people of different ethnic, cultural, sexual and religious orientation, while acknowledged, are still largely seen as the concern of small minorities. The emerging struggle of minority groups for equal rights and protection against discrimination in Ireland has its parallel in the feminist movement. After long and hard battles sexism is now at least recognised as existing, though we have not yet managed to free Irish society of sexist thinking and behaviour. Racism is still struggling to be recognised as an inequity.

Historically, Irish people have discriminated against and attacked the Jewish community, with incidents recorded in Cork and Dublin in the nineteenth century; including a pogrom in Limerick. More recently fascist groups have also indulged in anti-semitic activities, producing magazines and stickers which are abusive to Jews. Discrimination against Jews based on cultural differences is also common on an individual basis.

Ireland's missionary tradition has meant that Irish people have played their part in reinforcing and continuing the effects of colonialism mentioned earlier. While Irish missionaries have brought many positive things to the inhabitants of previously colonised countries, there is little doubt that the Christian churches, by introducing what they believed to be a superior code of beliefs, values, educational system, language and lifestyle, created an elitist and divisive structure within communities visited by missionary groups.

I come from Goa, a former Portuguese colony which in the sixties became part of India. St Francis Xavier, whose body is ceremoniously exposed each year on his feast day, brought Catholicism to Goa. As a child I read with fascination and horror about the Inquisition taking place in Goa at the same time as it did in Spain and Portugal, with its subsequent forced conversions. I assumed that the majority of Goans were Catholics, dominating as they did the social and institutional fabric of the region. With some surprise I discovered only in my early adulthood that two thirds of Goans were actually Hindus.

One of my worst experiences of racial discrimination, and one which I still find deeply painful to recall, was when I was between five and eight years of age, in a primary school run by an order of Irish nuns in India. The convent school was a fee-paying one and set in idyllic surroundings. Perhaps unintentionally, it contained a large proportion of white and 'Anglo-Indian' children. The white children were either resident or expatriate English or fair-skinned Parsis; the 'Anglo-Indian' children had some claim to superiority and whiteness through descent. There was little room for someone like me who was not only dark but, unfortunately (then), the darkest skinned in my class. My abiding memories of those years are the beauty of the place contrasted with the abysmal misery to which I was reduced by vicious taunting and endless bullying. The memory is relived each time I hear of a black child at school in Ireland being treated in a similar way.

My experience of racism in Ireland began as a student. In a small city where black women were virtually non-existent I was particularly conspicuous on and off campus. My middle-class, black femaleness was perceived as 'exotic', 'exciting', 'dangerous'. I was stared at, often to the point of rudeness, particularly when walking through the college canteen, a torture I soon gave up. I also stopped attending some lectures, for the same reason. My social relations with other students became limited and distorted. Those men who asked me out were seen as the 'daring few' and fell into three categories. The first were genuinely interested in me as a person; these were in a minority. The second, bluntly, were dominated by lascivious intent. The third, largely through ignorance, patronised or trivialised both my colour and my sex. Acute shyness, the strangeness of living in a new culture, and the lack of a clear understanding of how to deal with what I was encountering meant that, for the most part, I retreated into solitary loneliness. My feelings of inferiority and unacceptable 'difference' did not disappear when I began work in Ireland, or later when I married an Irishman; although by this

9

time my social milieu was largely accepting of me and therefore afforded me some protection against experiencing racism. I discovered that my knowledge of 'white' culture, whether literary, philosophical or historical, was assumed by those around me. However, the continuing significance or usefulness to me of my own culture and customs was of little interest to them. This sense of not belonging and of not being fully understood made me question for many years whether I had the right to bring a child, whose cultural origins would be as complex as my own, into such an unthinking society.

Ireland's traditional missionary role of proselytising has been largely replaced by charity and development work abroad. The approach to both is now generally more enlightened than when I first came to Ireland. I was horrified then to find school children still 'buying black babies'. The traditional missionary role and charity and development work are, however, fundamentally flawed by misconceptions.

There is still a belief underlying most Irish overseas development aid activities that we are not only better off but also more knowledgeable and intellectually or academically superior to people in third world countries. 'Black people are uncultured, ignorant, stupid and lazy and must be helped to think and do what is in their best interests.' Though this is no longer openly stated, it is difficult to gain any other impression from the publicity materials and campaigns launched by many fund-raising agencies in Ireland. Visual images and accounts of living conditions and disasters project black people as passive victims who do little or nothing for themselves. A few development organisations are attempting to return respect and responsibility to black people.

For the Irish development worker the existing construct poses a dilemma which is becoming more openly recognised. As one worker said in a recent newspaper interview: 'It is impossible to live and work ... without daily coming up against the racism inherent in both one's personal attitudes and in the nature of most aid programmes in the country ... On a personal level one tends to prejudge or classify people on the basis of colour. White is seen as wealthy, well-educated, powerful and "civilised", whereas black is considered to be poor, uneducated,

10

unimportant, simple and naïve ... These preconceived prejudices are usually only broken down by establishing real social relationships ...' (*Sunday Business Post*: 8 December 1991). The last sentence is particularly affecting. It can be difficult for development workers, who are invested, on arrival, with an innate superiority and who socialise within an expatriate network, to establish anything more than superficial relationships with local people. The elastoplast of do-gooding for so long the institutionalised and religious salve of the Irish conscience, is no longer seen as enough.

RACISM IN IRELAND TODAY

One often comes across the following line of argument in relation to racism in Ireland: if Irish people have unconsciously perpetrated racism overseas and continue to do so, it is understandable, one might say, given the historical context. At least Irish people are not racist in their own country today. Or they can't be since there is only a small number of black people in Ireland. So the argument and myth usually run. Firstly, the fact that there is a (small) indigenous black Irish population here is not usually recognised. Secondly, the resident black population of African, Asian and Middle-Eastern origin has increased in recent years, certainly much increased from the time I first arrived in Cork and was told by people that I was the first black woman they had ever met, the only black people they had met or seen having been male clerics.

While statistics and research are scant, there is no shortage of evidence of racism experienced by members of these minorities, both at the hands of institutions and in situations such as finding accommodation or employment. Unfortunately, organisations like Harmony, The Anti-Racist Coalition, and ICOS (Irish Council for Overseas Students) who monitor racist behaviour, do not have the resources to carry out much-needed research and to provide statistics.

Racist attitudes and behaviour against Travellers, Ireland's largest ethnic minority, are, however, well documented. Opinions amongst Irish people vary - one misconception being that all Travellers are descended from people who were

11

displaced from the land in the eighteenth and nineteeth centuries. Travellers are still not officially recognised as an ethnic minority, although the state has now implicitly recognised them as a distinct and identifiable group in recent legislation, notably The Prohibition of Incitement to Hatred Act which came into effect in 1990. Travellers have been discriminated against from as far back as the sixteenth century, when an Act was passed to prevent 'tynkers and pedlars' from moving from one town to another. At the time of writing, Dublin County Council is proposing to prevent Travellers from other parts of the country moving to Dublin. Such a proposal in relation to any other group of Irish residents, those from Cork or Sligo, would rightly be regarded as outrageous and would make news headlines.

There are an estimated 21,000 Travellers in Ireland, who have a distinct identity, culture and lifestyle, of which the characteristic of nomadism is the most controversial and the one least accepted by Irish people. It is usually referred to as the 'problem of itinerancy' or vagrancy and is viewed as illegal. The prejudice and discrimination against Travellers is similar to that practised by white people against black people. Travellers' skin colour does not protect them from racist thinking and behaviour, which is based on the ethnic and cultural differences between Travellers and 'settled' Irish people.

Let us first take the question of prejudice. How many of us personally know, socialise or can count a Traveller among our friends? Ask this question of the Irish in relation to black people. Many Irish people may never have seen a black person, owing to the small number of black people in Ireland. The same reason surely cannot be given for our lack of familiarity with Travellers. Yet generalisations about Travellers based on minimal contact abound. There are frequent protests by residents throughout the country whenever a halting site is to be built in their area. Generalisations, made on the basis of distant observations and myth, allow us to relinquish personal and collective responsibility for our society's behaviour towards marginalised groups.

Travellers are Irish and in some people's memories are regarded as part of the cultural fabric of rural Ireland where they went from place to place, working and then moving on. The collapse of the economic base of the Traveller community in the past thirty years has meant a shift from a rural to an urban base. This has resulted in an intensified experience of racism. Now, even though they are Irish citizens, Travellers are denied access to many of the basic rights accorded all citizens in relation to accommodation, education (less than twenty per cent of Traveller children attend secondary school), health, employment, social welfare, even the franchise. The Irish state makes it virtually impossible for Travellers to fully avail of these rights and still preserve their culture and lifestyle.

Institutionalised racism is illustrated by the statistics which reveal the systematic exclusion and oppression of travellers, eg, a high infant mortality rate, short life expectancy, frequent hospitalisation, high unemployment and widespread illiteracy.

Women Travellers bear a double burden of oppression. They are discriminated against by men who, as in settled society, hold the balance of power in the Traveller community. Discrimination which settled women experience in relation to education, employment and domestic labour is felt even more acutely by Traveller women. Traveller women, like settled women, bear the burden of domestic labour and responsibilities. Their domestic situation is made more difficult, however, by the quality of their accommodation and lack of access to water, sanitation, electricity, refuse collection, shops, launderettes and super-markets. Thus Traveller women are discriminated against by settled society and by Traveller males, while settled women fail to realise the common oppressions they share with their Traveller sisters.

HOW RACIST ARE IRISH INSTITUTIONS?

Institutional racism exists most visibly where racial discrimination is sanctioned by the constitution or laws of a country and legitimised in the authority of state institutions. The most extreme form of institutional racism is the apartheid system in South Africa which is now being slowly dismantled. This form of segregation, based on the colour of skin of different groups of people, led to a small (white) minority considering themselves superior to and holding economic and political power over the (black) majority. Another extreme form of racism is segregation of a minority to a limited area or territory, such as the reservations for Indians in North America, and homelands for the blacks of South Africa and aboriginal peoples of Australia.

Where does Ireland stand on anti-racist legislation? In the *Harmony Report: Racism in Ireland*, Marian Tannam states that 'In spite of having made human rights a central part of its own constitution, Ireland has played a disappointing role in the international human-rights movement. In 1971, Seán McBride commented that the failure to act then to become involved in the world struggle against racism "puts in question our sincerity when one professes loudly our attachment to the ideals of human liberty".'

Ireland has no comprehensive body of anti-discrimination legislation. The Prohibition to Incitement to Hatred Act (1990), makes it illegal for neo-Nazi and fascist groups to prepare or possess materials or recordings of a racist or similarly offensive nature in Ireland. Until then Ireland was being used as a base from which to publish and distribute such material to Europe. The passing of this Act enabled Ireland to belatedly ratify two International Covenants - one on Economic, Social and Cultural Rights (1966) and one on Civil and Political Rights (1966).

However, Ireland is still not in a position to ratify the *UN Convention on the Elimination of All Forms of Racial Discrimination* which it signed in 1968, and which, if ratified, would mean that individuals and groups in Ireland would be afforded legal protection against discrimination.

An Anti-Discrimination Bill being prepared by The Irish Travellers Movement, the Dublin Travellers Education and Development Group (DTEDG), and The Irish Council for Civil Liberties (ICCL) will be submitted to the Department of Justice in 1992. The Bill, while focusing on the Travellers, aims to set out the principle of equality for all groups. The Labour Party has published a Private Members Bill on Equal Status. The aim of the Bill is to outlaw discrimination against individuals and groups on any grounds including sex, colour, race, nationality, ethnic origin, disability, age and sexual orientation, with the exception of positive discrimination. Existing equality legislation in relation to employment refers only to sex-based discrimination and does not extend to discrimination on the basis of ethnic or cultural differences. The EEA (Employment Equality Agency) has no remit in this area.

ALIENS, IMMIGRANTS, REFUGEES AND THE DEPARTMENT OF JUSTICE

Irish immigration law is governed by the Aliens Act (1935) and the Irish Nationality Acts (1956) and (1986). These Acts establish two categories of persons - citizens and aliens. Anyone who does not fulfil the conditions for citizenship within the terms of the Irish Nationality Acts is in the residual category of aliens.

The Aliens Act and subsequent orders and regulations virtually determine the status, rights and obligations of aliens in this country. There are relatively few legislative Acts that discriminate against legally resident aliens; those which do, affect political participation, jury service, and entry to officership in the defence forces.

The situation is different in relation to immigrants. The Department of Justice has very wide discretion under The Aliens Act to enforce, by orders and regulations, restrictions on the entry, landing, freedom of movement, expulsion and deportation of aliens in the state.

In the late 1980s there was an increase in immigrant litigation in this country which focused on the constitutional rights of aliens, many of whom relied on the family law provisions of the Constitution, culminating in a landmark Supreme Court judgement in the case of *Fajujonu v. The Minister for Justice. 1990*. In this case an infant plaintiff, an Irish citizen, sued the Minister for an infringement of her family rights under the Constitution. The alleged infringement was the making of a deportation order against her father who was an alien. The Supreme Court held unanimously that 'where an alien has lived for an appreciable time in the state and has become a member of a family within the state containing children who are Irish citizens, those children have a Constitutional right to the company, care and parentage of their parents within that family'.

The judgment went on to say that where a family is constituted of alien parents and children who are Irish citizens, the state can force the family to leave only if it is satisfied that the interests of the common good and the protection of the state and society are so predominant and overwhelming as to justify such an interference.

The *Fajujonu* judgement is significant for two reasons. Until then there was a belief that where a policy question was involved natural justice and fundamental rights would be less likely to apply. The judgement also laid down for the first time that where the Department of Justice finds against the plaintiffs, reasons must be provided for the decision.

International Agreements concerning refugees have not been given effect in Irish law. All applications for refugee status and political asylum are determined by the Department of Justice. No information is available as to what criteria the Department applies to applications for refugee status and political asylum. There are no clear, public and enforceable procedures in relation to refugees, and the Irish refugee or asylum-seeker has no protection under Irish law.

There are an estimated 400 Vietnamese here, some refugees from Chile, and a very small group of Iranian Bahais. None of these refugees has entered the country through the discretion of the Department of Justice. They are here consequent to special invitation from the Minister of Foreign Affairs and international pressure.

INFLUENCE OF EDUCATION AND THE MEDIA

Two other institutions play a major role in fostering racism: the education system and the media. Both need to be considered in the light of *who* has access to them and *what* information and messages they choose to transmit.

Where access to education is concerned, I have already pointed out that less than twenty per cent of Traveller children attend secondary school. Education currently provided in many Irish schools neither affirms nor addresses the distinct identity of

Travellers, nor does it challenge the racism that Travellers experience.

The prevailing ethos in primary, secondary and third level schools and colleges is as inherently racist as it is sexist. The formal curriculum itself, particularly in the areas of history and geography, needs to be closely examined and overhauled. In Ireland today, it is possible to do a primary degree in history and never once in three years discuss racism or western colonial exploitation, even in relation to the racism Irish people have experienced as part of their own history, never mind that experienced by third world countries.

To really combat racism in the education system, new inter-cultural materials need to be introduced. Innovative ways of teaching, which bring pupils into contact with ethnic and cultural minorities, should be devised, ways which emphasise positive rather than negative aspects. At present there is little that helps to educate students about these differences; still less that ensures that the thinking of future generations will be permeated with anti-racist awareness and practice as surely as it is permeated with racist thinking at present.

To bring about such a change requires political will, resources and understanding of our global interdependency. Apart from the DTEDG there is hardly any organisation in Ireland providing specific anti-racist materials for schools. Some overseas development organisations state that there is an underlying anti-racist ethos in their development education materials which challenge assumptions about third world countries and other minorities. Many of the recommendations of the European Parliament *Report on Racism and Xenophobia,* deal with action the EC should take in combating racism through education. The Report recommends that:

Member states introduce teaching against racism into the curriculum of their primary schools as a compulsory subject (Recommendation 71).

Member States step up the support that education can provide for the campaign against racism, anti-semitism and xenophobia through the teaching of human rights and history at

17

school, through teacher training and university research (Recommendation 73).

There is no code of practice on racism and the media in Ireland. *Guide-lines on Race Reporting* are, however, issued to NUJ (National Union of Journalists) members in Britain. It has been said that the media are not directly racist in their reporting of news items in Ireland, though individual instances of racist reporting have been documented. However, implicit in much media reporting and advertising, when closely scrutinised, is the continued assumption that western culture is superior and black culture is inferior. It is evident in reports on political regimes which western cultures find unacceptable and in so-called documentaries where women, particularly, are often portrayed as subservient with little or no social, economic or political independence, in sharp contrast to the 'liberated' western woman who may well be doing the reporting.

Juxtapositions of this kind are particularly noticeable in advertising and fashion features on television and in magazines, where visual images convey the sophistication of the 'white' woman in contrast to the 'primitive nature' of the blacks surrounding her. A favourite image is that of the vulnerable white woman, more often than not dressed in virginal white, with the presence of a black man nearby or in the background, implying threat or danger. Such images are inextricably invested with highly charged sexual, racial or class meanings. They might not set out to be explicitly racist, but they are part of a familiar everyday imagery through which racism is expressed.

In order to establish how balanced and fair media coverage is in relation to ethnic groups, the information and images transmitted about, to and from ethnic groups need to be examined. No such analysis of the Irish media has ever been undertaken.

The *Evrigenis Report* maintains that: 'Information about minorities is quite often biased, dwelling at length on the misdemeanours of some members of minority groups, giving poor coverage to the problems of such communities and ignoring almost all their achievements ...' It continues: 'Whilst acknowledging that the media can play a positive role in forming knowledge about ethnic communities, it is undeniable that currently overall media presentation perpetuates a negative image of these communities.' The Report then recommends 'that a campaign be conducted to raise the awareness of media professionals of the importance of their role in eliminating racial and xenophobic prejudices, particularly through appropriate treatment of the news'.

IRELAND WITHIN THE EC

The advent of a single European market within the EC is supposed to allow the freedom of movement of goods, services and people within the Member States. This entails harmonisation of policies and legislation. Harmonisation of policies in relation to freedom of movement has become a contentious issue. Racism is increasing in Europe and there is also a marked increase in neo-Nazi and fascist movements. This has been matched by an increase in representation of democratically elected extreme right-wing parties in many EC countries. In Germany, members of ethnic groups have been moved into hostels in large numbers to protect them from violent attacks. In Britain, where 7,000 racial attacks are reported a year, it is estimated that there is under-reporting of attacks by a factor of ten. The *Eurobarometer* survey on racism in 1989 found that one in three Europeans felt that there were too many non-nationals in their country. A sizeable minority felt the presence of immigrants in their country was a negative factor for the future. At the same time, one in four EC citizens were in favour of improving or at least maintaining the rights of immigrants. Most people were in favour of harmonising immigration legislation within the Community, rather than Member States making unilateral decisions in relation to immigrants.

While on the face of it harmonisation seems to make good sense, there is a fear among many that it will lead to more restrictive policies being practised by some Member States in preference to the more liberal ones of others. In bringing about harmonisation, international conventions, inter-governmental coordination and human-rights issues are of key importance.

The main groups working on inter-governmental coordination on harmonisation are the TREVI (Terrorism, Radicalism, Extremism and Violence Initiative) and the Rhodes Groups. Both groups have come under considerable criticism from anti-racist organisations. The TREVI Group, originally set up to combat terrorism, proposed standardised solutions for policing national frontiers which included regular checks on migrants, refugees and asylum seekers. The Rhodes Group arbitrarily drew up a list of fifty-nine countries whose nationals it decided would require an entry visa for any of the twelve Member States. They also excluded the UN High Commissioner for Refugees from discussions within the group of coordinators when refugee matters were being discussed, in violation of both the Treaty of Rome and the UN Convention and Protocol on the Status of Refugees.

It has been mooted that a common immigration policy, while desirable, is not essential before internal frontiers are abolished, and that non-Europeans living in the EC would be able to circulate freely through the Community although they would not always have the right of residence. It is difficult to see how this distinction could be made, without creating a stratum of second-class citizens who, without nationality but legally resident in a Member State, would be more vulnerable to random identity controls because of their skin colour. One has only to go through Dublin airport any day of the week to see that this situation already exists, with black people being regularly singled out for identity checks.

The twelve Member States of the European Community have a total population of 320 million. Approximately six million of these are from developing countries. The Federal Republic of Germany (FRG), pre-unification, had the highest percentage - 5.2 per cent of non EC migrants. Ireland and Italy have the lowest with 0.5 per cent and 0.2 per cent respectively. Known incidents of harassment and violence in Ireland are low compared to some other countries but, considering the small number of groups of people here from other countries, it is not particularly encouraging. Rather, it is felt that if there were more foreigners here, particularly non-Europeans, 'racism and xenophobia could reach dangerous levels' *(Report on the*

Findings of the Committee of Inquiry into Racism and Xenophobia, 1991).

Racism not only exists but is a major social, moral and political problem in Europe. It is up to each of us to deal with our individual ignorance, fear and racist tendencies. Collectively, we need actively to influence the role Ireland plays in ensuring that we live in a society which respects fundamental rights and rejects all forms of discrimination.

FOSTERING RACISM

Cultural roots do not necessarily and simply mean belonging to a particular country, city, town or community. They are an internal state, an inner-self. As children we develop a data-bank or blueprint of family memories, experiences, symbols, commitments and values. These we apply to individuals, places, lifestyles and shared moral and social mores. Our individual culture becomes a map of meaning which helps us to make sense of our lives. We identify with the culture or distinctive way of life of a group or class, as it is manifested in institutions, social relations, systems of belief, the use of objects and materials. All these are initially invested with the meanings, values and ideas of our blueprint. With increased experience, knowledge, and exposure to new things and people, we add or subtract from the subscribed norms of the blueprint. As we grow older, we graft our own memories and experiences on to it. The childhood blueprint is our essential repository, our most inner self. But it evolves as our ideas, beliefs, and values change and as we ally with like-minded people within a local, national or more extensive global framework. Thus, culture is not a static mantle of values, beliefs and behaviour but a mixture of all that we have experienced and thought about that makes life meaningful to us.

This has particular personal relevance for me as a black woman born in India with a mixed Portuguese, British and Indian culture, who has chosen to spend my adult life in Ireland and raise a family here. Skin colour and sexism have been paramount in the evolving of my blueprint. My inner-self has been defined and constantly redefined by and for me, in relation to the 'superior white other'. Being perceived as inferior has left me with an abiding sense of inadequacy and guilt which is only slowly decreasing. I have often been subjected to a type of inverted racism which disregards the cultures which have formed me. Because I am middle class, do not speak English with a broken accent and do not wear any particular national costume, I am often regarded as 'not really Indian', 'not Irish', a 'West Brit', 'not coloured, because you're like us'. What is perceived as an identifying feature about me is used, consciously or unconsciously, to discriminate by either inclusion or exclusion. There is an assumption among many Irish people that those whose skin colour is different 'aspire' to adopt a 'superior, less primitive' culture.

Each of our identities is made up of an intertwining of such factors as ethnic origin, culture, class and gender. To discuss any one of these characteristics in isolation without reference to the others is to grossly over-simplify the complexity and enormity of the discrimination problem.

Historically, the struggles of black people and women for emancipation are related. White women initially looked at the slavery of black people in order to understand and interpret their own domination. Parallels and comparisons of subordination were drawn. American feminists in the 1960s adopted much of the language and non-violent tactics of black activists in the civil rights movement. These interconnections have since had an uneasy and often fraught alliance.

In Britain, a lack of true understanding of black women together with a focus on cultural customs such as the dowry system and arranged marriages have led to bitter divisions between white and Asian feminist women. Black women have experienced white feminists as quick to criticise and direct, but less keen to listen and learn. Black women have experienced the women's movement as narrow and reluctant to expand and incorporate other visions and realities.

The women's movement in Ireland has scarcely begun to address these issues. For me, the divisions which have characterised the politics of feminism in relation to black women first need to be recognised and then overcome. This can only be done if one moves from sympathy towards recognition of other realities, which in turn will lead to the formation of alliances to lend weight to political actions. Thus, in Ireland, Traveller and black women need to ally with settled white women to achieve solidarity and strength in order to win collective battles.

To do this we need actively to search out points of common reference and collaborate on shared actions and interactions. These must recognise and accept the differences, aims and ideals of all those who have been marginalised by the single, double and triple oppressions of class, gender and race.

REFERENCES AND FURTHER READING

Banton, M. and Harwood, J., *The Race Concept*. Newton Abbott: David and Charles, 1975.

Bourne, J., *Towards an Anti-Racist Feminism*. London: Institute of Race Relations, 1984.

Cashmore, E., *The Dictionary of Race and Ethnic Relations*. London: Routledge and Kegan Paul, 1984.

Community Workers Co-op., *Women and the Community*. Dublin: Co-options, 1989.

Community Workers Co-op., *Racism, Co-options*. Special Edition, Dublin: APSO, 1990.

Committee of Inquiry into Racism and Xenophobia, *Report on the Findings of the Inquiry*. Luxembourg, 1991.

The Courier, *Dossier: Immigration*. Number 129, 1991.

Crowley, N., *Racism and the Travellers*. Dublin: DTEDG, 1991.

Eager, B., *The Situation of Aliens, Migrants and Nomads in Ireland*. Dublin: DTEDG, 1991.

Evrigenis Report, European Parliament working document report, Document A2-160/85, Luxembourg, 1985.

Eurobaromenter, *Public Opinion in the European Community*. Special Edition on Racism and Xenophobia, Brussels: EC, 1989.

European Parliament, *Report on Racism and Xenophobia*, 1991.

Harmony Report, *Racial Discrimination in Ireland: Realities and Remedies*. March, 1990.

Husband, C. ed., *Race in Britain - Community and Change*. London: Hutchinson, 1982.

Links 21, *White Lies - Racism and Underdevelopment*. Oxford: Third World First, 1984.

Miles, R. and Phizachlea, A., *White Man's Country: Racism and British Politics*. London: Pluto Press, 1984.

NGO-EC Liaison Committee, *Code of Conduct - Images and Messages Relating to the Third World*. Brussels, 1989.

Olé, Olé, Olé, - Racism in Dublin. In Dublin: 2-15 August, 1990.

Pontifical Commission, 'Iustitia et Pax.' *The Church and Racism - Towards a More Fraternal Society*. Dublin: Veritas, 1989.

Tannam, M., *Racism in Ireland - Sources of Information*. Dublin: Harmony, 1991.

UN, International Convention on the Elimination of All Forms of Racial Discrimination, 1965.

UNESCO, *Sociological Theories. Race and Colonialism*. Paris: Unesco, 1980.

Ware, V., *Beyond the Pale - White Women, Racism and History*. London: Verso, 1992.

ACKNOWLEDGEMENTS

Thank you to all those who gave me information and support, particularly to APSO, the Agency for Personal Service Overseas; Róisín Conroy, Gráinne Healy, Ailbhe Smyth and all at Attic Press; Niall Crowley, John O'Connell, Killian O'Donnell, Vivienne Rooney and my closest collaborator, Lynnea Fitzgerald.